Learning CoreOS

Guide for Beginners

Table of Contents

Introduction

Containers are a common way of running and managing applications in today's world. They make the work of managing easy for us. We can easily secure, update, and simplify the container infrastructure with CoreOS. It helps us setup the clusters we need to use, and these clusters will all be managed as a single unit. The good thing with CoreOS containers is that they can be run on a massive scale, and you will experience minimum or no overhead at all. CoreOS is very flexible, which makes it possible for us to run it on various platforms. This book guides you on how to use CoreOS. Enjoy reading!

Chapter 1- What is CoreOS?

CoreOS is a Linux distribution which helps us setup and run clustered environments easily and quickly. It helps us to manage clusters as a single unit. This distribution was developed based on the Chrome OS, and it helps us to maintain a host system which is lightweight, and makes use of a Docker container in all applications.

With this system, you can isolate processes. The container was designed so that it can run on a massive scale, with no or minimal operation overhead. Container Linux applications usually run in containers and the developer is provided with tools for easy deployment of software.

The container Linux is capable of running on any container platform, may it be virtual, physical, public, or private. CoreOS helps you achieve security, automation, and scalability of your applications.

Chapter 2- Setting up a Cluster

The CoreOS operating system can be run in a variety of different applications. The CoreOS has a coreos-vagrant repository in the GitHub, which provides a solid basis on which one can setup and then run a cluster within minutes. Let us use this cluster so as to make a local CoreOS cluster.

First, ensure that you have installed the following:

1. VirtualBox
2. Vagrant

If you have not installed git, open the coreos-vagrant repository, and download its source code as an archived file. Unpack the downloaded file, and then change your directory to the folder which you have just unpacked. If you had already installed the git, just clone the coreos-vagrant repository, and then change the directory to it. Now that you have VirtualBox and Vagrant installed, we can go ahead to set up the cluster.

Configuration

The use of CoreOS only becomes useful in situations where you are running not less than three machines. It is only in such cases thst you are able to benefit from one of the goals of CoreOS, which is high-availability. When you run a cluster having only 2 machines, the CoreOS will find it hard to make a decision on the leader. These two machines will submit their vote and there will be a tie of 50-50, hence unable to decide on who will be the leader.

In CoreOS, the “etcd” is used for connecting machines in the cluster. Also, with the etcd, the leader is chosen automatically. If a machine is not a leader in the cluster, it becomes a follower, and it will be able to accept the role of a leader in case the leader fails due to issues such as the hardware failure.

Get the Etcd Discovery Token

Etcd makes use of a discovery token so as to quickly spin a cluster. It also uses an existing cluster so as to create a new cluster, and gets a cluster token from an available one so that it can establish connections between the machines within the cluster.

It is possible for you to use the etcd functionality which exists on the etcd cluster of CoreOS. They will show the URL from which a new discovery token can be obtained from the already existing cluster. The size of the new cluster has to be predefined. In case you fail to put the proper cluster size as part of the query parameter when using the CoreOS's discovery cluster, then a default size of 3 will be used.

When you use the URL given below, you can be able to get a cluster size of 3. The token value will be the alphanumeric string located at the end of the URL which is returned. Here is the URL:

https://discovery.etcd.io/new

The size of the cluster should be passed as a query parameter at the end of the URL. You should add the parameter "?size=n," whereby n should be replaced with the size of the cluster that you want to have. In our case, we want to use a cluster size of 4, so we should have the following URL:

https://discovery.etcd.io/new?size=4

The above will return a URL which has a discovery token. This is shown below:

https://discovery.etcd.io/538fb2b0a1ff50075e170080066c8647

The discovery UL will then be used in the "#cloud-config." Let us discuss the #cloud-config in more detail.

Cloud-Config

The CoreOS makes use of Cloud-Config so as to configure the parameters for machines and services and for launching the system units during the system boot. The coreos-vagrant repository has the file "user-data.sample" which has a predefined "#cloud-config" content The project is capable of recognizing the file user-data located inside the directory. This is an indication that you should copy the "user-data.sample" file to the "user-data" or imply create a new user-data file. The "user-data" file in our case should have the content given below:

#cloud-config

coreos:
etcd2:
 # generate a new token for each unique cluster
 # from https://discovery.etcd.io/new?size=n where n = cluster size

 # discovery url to bootstrap the cluster
discovery:
https://discovery.etcd.io/538fb2b0a1ff50075e17008006c8647
 # multi-region and multi-cloud deployments need to use $public_ipv4

 # list of member's client urls to advertise information to the rest of the cluster

advertise-client-urls: http://$public_ipv4:2379
 # this address is used to communicate etcd data around the cluster

initial-advertise-peer-urls: http://$private_ipv4:2380

```
  # listen on both the official ports and the legacy ports
  # legacy ports can be omitted if your application doesn't depend on them

  # url to listen for client traffic
  listen-client-urls: http://0.0.0.0:2379,http://0.0.0.0:4001
  # url to listen for peer traffic
  listen-peer-urls: http://$private_ipv4:2380,http://$private_ipv4:7001

 fleet:
  public-ip: $public_ipv4
 flannel:
  interface: $public_ipv4
 units:
  - name: etcd2.service
    command: start
  - name: fleet.service
    command: start
```

In case you try to copy the contents of the above files and then use them in your project, just ensure that you have changed the value of the discovery token to the value you have in your project. The variables "$private_ipv4" and "$public_ipv4" should work as substitution variables, and Vagrant will replace them with the actual values for the machine.

config.rb

The coreos-vagrant basic repository comes with the file "config.rb.sample" which can help do some further configurations on your cluster.

There is no need for you to copy “config.rb.sample” to the “config.rb,” so then go ahead and do some further configurations. The only thing which needs to be changed is the number of the cluster machine instances which are contained in the cluster. The value for the cluster size should be defined within the Vagrantfile.

Vagrantfile

If you are experienced with working with Vagrant, you must be aware of the syntax and the options in the Vagrantfile, and you know how to configure the machine so as to meet your needs.

The coreos-vagrant repository has vagrantfile, which is somewhat complex, and this is the reason why you should be aware of some of the fundamentals so as to understand what is happening with your machine.

However, for those who don’t need to interfere with the Vagrantfiles options, just open the file. We will change only two values and then kick off the cluster. Find the following variables within the Vagrantfile, and then change them:

$num_instances = 5
$update_channel = "stable"

The variable “$num_instances” is used for defining the size of the cluster. This has been set to 5, which means that we will start 5 etcd instances, although we had set this to 4 while getting the discovery token. This gives us an extra coreos instance, and this will be used as the proxy node by default.

The CoreOS provides us with three update channels which include stable, beta, and alpha. When you are spinning up the cluster, the type of channel you choose is not a determinant factor.

Start the Cluster

The basic configuration which is necessary for the core cluster to get started is now finished. By use of the default vagrant provider for VirtualBox, we have to use the “vagrant up” command so as to launch the cluster. This command should run as shown below:

$ vagrant up
Bringing machine 'core-01' up with 'virtualbox' provider...

Bringing machine 'core-02' up with 'virtualbox' provider...

Bringing machine 'core-03' up with 'virtualbox' provider...

Bringing machine 'core-04' up with 'virtualbox' provider...

Bringing machine 'core-05' up with 'virtualbox' provider...

==> core-01: Importing base box 'coreos-stable'...
==> core-01: Matching MAC address for NAT networking...

==> core-01: Checking if box 'coreos-stable' is up to date...

==> core-01: A newer version of the box 'coreos-stable' is available! You currently

==> core-01: have version '717.3.0'. The latest is version '723.3.0'. Run

==> core-01: `vagrant box update` to update.

```
==> core-01: Setting the name of the VM: coreos-vagrant_core-01_1448937703037_3422

==> core-01: Clearing any previously set network interfaces...

==> core-01: Preparing network interfaces based on configuration...

    core-01: Adapter 1: nat
    core-01: Adapter 2: hostonly
==> core-01: Forwarding ports...
    core-01: 22 => 2222 (adapter 1)
==> core-01: Running 'pre-boot' VM customizations...
==> core-01: Booting VM...
...
```

Once the 5 machines within the cluster have been created and then started by Vagrant, you may run the following command so as to check for the status:

```
$ vagrant status
Current machine states:

core-01                  running (virtualbox)
core-02                  running (virtualbox)
core-03                  running (virtualbox)
core-04                  running (virtualbox)
core-05                  running (virtualbox)
```

This environment represents multiple VMs. The VMs are all listed above with their current state. For more information about a specific VM, run `vagrant status NAME`.

The machine is now running. We can now check for the status of the machine and the cluster from the fleet and etcd.

If you need to sh into any of the machines you have created and booted, just use the “vagrant ssh <machine-name>” command.

Cluster Members

The etcd is the one tasked with the responsibility of connecting all the machines contained in a cluster. It is responsible for storing the information about the cluster and choosing the appropriate leader.

The command given below is being executed from the CoreOS system. Just perform a SSH into any of the available machines and then run the commands. To show the list of the available cluster members, just run the “etcd member list” command. You should inspect to ensure that each machine was joined in the right way during boot up. This is shown below:

$ etcdctl member list
bc165403c23a8872:
name=01a2ce2426014b6285fc87dc9c2ff8b0
peerURLs=http://172.17.8.100:2380
clientURLs=http://172.17.8.101:2379

bd23d18de5cae135:
name=ce70e12e334045469a392d1900a6f0dd
peerURLs=http://172.17.8.102:2380
clientURLs=http://172.17.8.103:2379

e25b97626ae78a1d:
name=ca89e84c086e4b459fec4d9b458b1e6b
peerURLs=http://172.17.8.103:2380
clientURLs=http://172.17.8.104:2379

ecd855606dbfcd02:
name=c919f394360c4fa78f518f28562af511
peerURLs=http://172.17.8.102:2380
clientURLs=http://172.17.8.102:2379

Our list will then print four cluster members. During the process of getting the discovery token, we had defined a cluster size of 4. The etcd will allow four tokens to automatically join the cluster, and any other additional machine will have to fall back into the proxy node.

Machines in a Cluster

Since we had created a total of 5 CoreOS machines, we should check whether all our nodes have been booted correctly and that they are running correctly. Although we have 4 machines in the cluster, we have 1 proxy node which stays in the etcd's information loop. All the etcd cluster data will be passed to a proxy node.

You should make use of the "fleetctl" command line utility so as to show the list of all the available machines. This is shown below:

$ fleetctl list-machines --full=true

This will list all the machines which are available for you. The "--full=true" option is responsible for showing the full id for each machine. With this, it will be easy for us to compare the machines which are generally available to the ones in the etcd cluster.

When you are starting the CoreOS, the Etcd, and the fleet, you may encounter an issue that the etcd couldn't connect to the cluster or the other machines.

$ fleetctl list-machines
Error retrieving list of active machines: googleapi: Error 503: fleet server unable to communicate with etcd

This makes it hard to get the machines which are connected to each other. Remember that we failed to keep track of the following:

When copying "user-data.sample" to "user-data,",\ a config definition exists for the etcd and etcd2. Each new CoreOS comes with etcd2. You can confirm within "#cloud-config" whether you started etcd2 and delete etcd lines.

If your cluster does not have enough machines, then this may also be a cause for the error. The number of available machines should not be less than what you specified during the process of getting the discovery token.

Chapter 3- Running Node.js Apps on the Cluster

Creating Docker App Container

The docker container can be created in a number of ways. You must have heard about DOCKERFILES and how to use the command line for creating the container. You will learn to use the command line and make the creation of the container more flexible. You can also use the DOCKERFILE so as to create the container.

We will be using Ubuntu 14.04 as the base image. Run the command given below so as to create your initial Docker container:

docker run -i -t ubuntu:14.04 /bin/bash

Let us explain the parameters which have been used in the command given above:

- **run:** tells the docker to launch a container with the parameter given and depending on the given base image.

- **-i:** tells the docker to launch the container in an interactive mode and it makes the STDIN of the container available.

- **-t:** tells the docker to create a pseudo-TTY session. This will gives us access to the terminal of the docker container which is running Ubuntu.

- **ubuntu:14.04:** this is a combination of the repository:image. We are using a ubuntu repository with the base image 14.04.

- **/bin/bash::** the command we need to execute inside a container. Since we need to install some tools, we need access to the command line and then to spawn a shell session.

Note that you can choose to run the command from any of your available CoreOS machines. Note that Docker comes with CoreOS already installed. The command can be executed within the local machine. In case you have created a Docker in your local machine, then ensure that the Container has been installed in your system.

After submitting the command to the local machine or CoreOS, you will get an output which looks like the one given below:

$ docker run -i -t ubuntu:14.04 /bin/bash
Unable to find image 'ubuntu:14.04' locally
14.04: Pulling from library/ubuntu
0bf056161913: Downloading [>] 539.8 kB/65.67 MB
1796d1c62d0c: Download complete
e24428725dd6: Download complete

The Docker base image which you define will be pulled from the Docker Hub in case it is not found locally. However, you have to be patient, as the process of downloading the base image to your local system may take a lot of time.

Once the base image has been completely downloaded, you will be taken to the terminal session of your Docker container.

At this point, we will have access to our Ubuntu Shell, and we can make use of the package manager which "apt" so as to repositories and install the Node.js and curl. We will make use of Nodesource packages which have to be fetched by curl before the installation of Node.js can be done. Run the following sequence of commands in your container so as to install Node.js:

```
apt-get update
apt-get install -y curl
curl -sL https://deb.nodesource.com/setup_4.x | sudo -E bash -

apt-get install -y nodejs
```

You can then check for NVM and Node versions by running the following commands:

```
$ node -v
$ npm –v
```

We can now go ahead, and then create our actual app.

Creating the App

We now want to demonstrate how you can create and then run a Node.js app within the CoreOS cluster. To do this, we should begin by creating a basic Node.js server which is capable of responding to each request with a message. We need to read a value from etcd and then respond to our requests by use of a view which shows the real value or a default value.

Below we have the content for the file “server.js,” and it is a representation of the Node.js app. It is possible for you to run apps which are more complex in this way. The example will help you to understand how to get a Node.js submitted and then running on a CoreOS cluster.

The files server.json and package.json will be placed in the /src folder. We will have chosen a folder in which to install our dependencies and know from where we can launch the server during submission and launching it on the cluster. Here is the code for the file “server.js”:

```
const http = require('http')
const Etcd = require('node-etcd')
```

```
const etcd = new Etcd('172.17.8.102', '4001')

const hostname = '0.0.0.0'
// this will expose Node.js server beyond the
localhost. This should be

// avoided in production!
const port = 3000

http.createServer((req, res) => {
 etcd.get(req.url.slice(1), function (err, result) {
  res.writeHead(200, { 'Content-Type': 'text/plain' })
  if (err) {
     console.log(err)
     res.end('No value for key "' + req.url.slice(1) + '"
available in the etcd')

  } else {
     res.end('Got value for key "' + req.url.slice(1) + '"
from etcd: ' + result.node.value)

  }
 })
}).listen(port, hostname, () => {
 console.log('Server running at the url
http://${hostname}:${port}/')

})
```

The Node.js should then be initialized with NPM inside the Docker container by use of “npm init.” The NPM should then be told to use the file server.js as an entry point for the app. You can then use the “npm i -S node-etcd” so as to install the node-etcd. Lastly, run your app so as to see that everything is working as expected, while expecting to find that the server was started at 127.0.0.1 and by use of port 3000. This is shown below:

```
$ node server.js
```

Server running at http://127.0.0.1:3000/

Pushing the Image

We now have our Docker container readily prepared, and the Node.js application is running well. Our next step should be to commit and then push our image to the Docker Hub repositories.

For us to be able to commit the container, we must be aware of the image ID. Begin by listing all the containers which are available in your machine by running the command given below:

$ docker ps –l

Make sure that you have noted the ID of the container which you need to commit and then push to the repository. This calls for you to pay attention to the CONTAINER ID filed in the output. Below is the syntax for the Docker commit command:

docker commit <container id> <docker-hub-username>/<image-name>

You can then use the syntax given above and replace it with your details. In my case, this will be as shown below:

$ docker commit 497e20f53563 nicohsam/node-etcd

With that, we will have committed the changes, and it is now time for us to push the container image to the repository. Note that the process of uploading and distributing the image can take some time, so remain patient. The push command should be as follows:

$ docker push nicohsam/node-etcd

After the upload is complete, the container will be available via Docker Hub, and it will be possible for us to create a unit file which can help us to pull the image into the local machine which we will be using to host the app.

Creating Unit Files

We have our docker container ready for deployment and pushing to the Docker hub. This is an indication that we are ready for creation of the unit files which will be used for deployment purposes. We are going to create two unit files.

One will be named "node-etcd" which will boot the Docker container and then start the Node.js server inside our container. Secondly, we will create a unit file which will be used as a helper and for announcing the app service to the etcd.

node-etcd

The unit file usually describes itself. The [Unit] block in the file serves to explain that the unit is in need of docker and etcd so as to run as well as the dependency to the discovery service. In the [Service] block, we tell the fleet to do away with all the containers created previously with the name node-etcd%i, and the %i is just a placeholder for the port number to be passed when the service is starting. This is shown below:

[Unit]
Description=Node.js app inside a docker container reading a value from etcd

After=etcd2.service
After=docker.service
Requires=node-etcd-discovery@%i.service

[Service]
TimeoutStartSec=0

```
KillMode=none
EnvironmentFile=/etc/environment
ExecStartPre=-/usr/bin/docker kill node-etcd%i
ExecStartPre=-/usr/bin/docker rm node-etcd%i
ExecStartPre=/usr/bin/docker pull
marcuspoehls/node-etcd
ExecStart=/usr/bin/docker run --name node-etcd%i -
p %i:3000 \

  -P -e
COREOS_PRIVATE_IPV4=${COREOS_PRIVATE_IP
V4}      \

  nicohsam/node-etcd                    \
  /bin/sh -c "cd /src && npm i && node server.js" -D
FOREGROUND

ExecStop=/usr/bin/docker stop node-etcd%i

[X-Fleet]

Conflicts=node-etcd@*.service
```

Once we stop the service, the Docker will be told to stop the container. We also have the [X-Fleet] constraint which instructs the fleet to add this to each machine only once.

The "node-etcd-discovery"

This helper is responsible for announcing the Node.js app to other cluster members, and this is spread once the node-etcd service has been started. This has to be launched simultaneously, as it is a requirement for the node-etcd. There is no need for you to worry about the service "node-etcd-discovery," as the fleet will do this job on our behalf and start it beside the node-etcd. This is shown below:

```
[Unit]
```

```
Description=Announce node-etcd@%i service
BindsTo=node-etcd@%i.service

[Service]
EnvironmentFile=/etc/environment
ExecStart=/bin/sh -c "while true; do etcdctl set
/announce/services/node-etcd%i
${COREOS_PUBLIC_IPV4}:%i --ttl 60; sleep 45;
done"

ExecStop=/usr/bin/etcdctl rm
/announce/services/node-etcd%i

[X-Fleet]
MachineOf=node-etcd@%i.service
```

Once the service “node-etcd” has stopped, the fleet will go ahead to remove the announcement from etcd. The [X-Fleet] condition is responsible for binding “node-etcd-discovery” to node-etcd. This service is launched in the same machine as the node-etcd launches.

Running Node.js App on the CoreOS Cluster

This should be the final step, and we will see the Node.js app running on the CoreOS cluster.

We should begin by submitting the services node-etcd and node-etcd-discovery to the cluster by use of fleetctl. The following commands can help us achieve this:

```
$ fleetctl submit node-etcd@.service node-etcd-discovery@.service

Unit node-etcd@.service inactive
Unit node-etcd-discovery@.service inactive

$ fleetctl list-unit-files
UNIT                    HASH    DSTATE   STATE
TARGET

hello.service           f55c0ae  loaded   loaded
4781dfef.../172.17.8.102

node-etcd-discovery@.service  d8c5ae5  inactive
inactive  -
node-etcd@.service      c48c872  inactive  inactive
-
```

From the result given above, it is very clear that things ran smoothly. The services are now available in the init system of the cluster, and their state is inactive. That was our expectation, since we have submitted them without following any service start.

We now need to move the unit to the server. The "fleetctl" will follow and respect the constraints which have been defined in the [X-Fleet] block in unit files. Since we had specified that the service "node-etcd-discovery" should run aside the node-etcd service, these services should be expected to load on a similar machine. If you need a shortcut to this procedure, you only have to launch the "node-etcd" service, and the service loading will be handled by the fleet. This is shown below:

$ fleetctl load node-etcd@3000.service
Unit node-etcd@3000.service inactive
Unit node-etcd@3000.service loaded on 665d4315.../172.17.8.102

$ fleetctl load node-etcd-discovery@3000.service
Unit node-etcd-discovery@3000.service inactive
Unit node-etcd-discovery@3000.service loaded on 665d4315.../172.17.8.102

As shown above, both the services were submitted to the machine by use of a trailing IP, which is .102. At the point, we are very close to the running of the Node.js server. The unit files we have have specified that the service "node-etcd-discovery" should bind to the actual node-etcd service. This is an indication that we are capable of starting the node-etcd service, while the fleet will take the responsibility of starting both. This is shown below:

$ fleetctl start node-etcd@3000.service
Unit node-etcd@3000.service launched on 665d4315.../172.17.8.102

fleetctl list-units
UNIT MACHINE ACTIVE SUB

hello.service 2381dfde.../172.17.8.103 inactive dead

node-etcd-discovery@3000.service 665d4315.../172.17.8.102 active running

node-etcd@3000.service 665d4315.../172.17.8.102 active running

This looks okay, with both node-etcd* services being in an active and running state. We should now verify whether we are in a position to access the server.

Now that we have our Node.js app started on the CentOS server, we can check whether we are in a position to access the app via the browser. Make use of the IP address of your server in which the service was loaded and then started on. In this case, this should be the server whose IP address is 172.17.8.102. Just launch the browser, and then access the Node.js server on port 3000, since the port 3000 had been forwarded from the docker container to the host machine.

Chapter 4- Kubernetes with CoreOS on the AWS

In this chapter, we will guide you on how to run your kebernetes cluster on the Amazon Web Services (AWS).

Setup kube-aws

Install this by running the following command:

$ wget https://github.com/coreos/coreos-**kubernetes/releases/download/v0.8.3/kube-aws-linux-amd64.tar.gz**

$ tar zxvf kube-aws-linux-amd64.tar.gz
$ sudo mv linux-amd64/kube-aws /usr/local/bin

First, we used the "wget" command for downloading the packaged. Note that the packaged comes in a zipped format. We then used the "tar" command so as to unzip it.

AWS CLI and Authentication

Before we can begin to use the *"KUBE-AWS," WE SHOULD FIRST INSTALL THE AWS CLI AND BE AUTHENTICATED TO AWS WITH IT. TO VERIFY WHETHER THE AUTHENTICATION HAD BEEN DONE, JUST RUN THE* "aws ec2 describe-instances" command. If this has not been done, then you will have to provide your necessary credentials as well as the AWS region which you need to use. The following example demonstrates how this can be:

$aws configure
AWS Access Key ID [None]: BKID25397678236
AWS Secret Access Key [None]: YOUR-SECRET-KEY
Default region name [None]: us-west-2
Default output format [None]: text

In the above example, the parameters AWS Access Key ID and the AWS Secret Access Key refers to the credentials of the user who has the necessary permissions to setup all the above.

Preconfiguring AWS Resources

The following are the AWS resources which are mandatory, and you must prepare them in the AWS:

- EC2 key pair which will be used.
- KMS key (Encryption key).
- External DNS name.

The EC2 Key pair

You can find EC2 key pairs under the EC2 section in the AWS Web GUI. For you to create a new key pair, just run the following command:

aws ec2 create-key-pair --key-name YourKeyPair

If you have an existing public key, just upload it if you need to.

The AWS KMS

You may need to use a different key for the kubernetes. You may also have never used an encryption key before. To create one, run the following command:

aws kms --region=<your-region> create-key --description="kube-aws assets"

The command will then give you the new key's arn.

DNS name for accessing the cluster

There is a need for you to define the DNS host name in which you will be in a position to access the cluster API. We will then make use of this hostname for the purpose of provisioning the TLS certificate for our API server.

After the creation of the cluster, the TLS-secured API will be exposed by the controller on a public IP address. You will then be expected to create a record for your chosen DNS hostname which needs to be pointed to the IP address.

Initializing the asset directory

At this point, we have everything ready for the creation of the asset directory.

**kube-aws init **
**--cluster-name=kube-dev **
**--external-dns-name=kube.domain.com **
**--region=eu-central-1 **

```
--availability-zone=eu-central-1a \
--key-name=id_aws \
--kms-key-arn="arn:aws:kms:eu-central-1:688657842227:key/xxxxxxxxxxxxxxxxxxxxxxxxxxxxxxxxxxxx"
```

The above code will create a file named "cluster.yaml," which will be based on the initial values. You should check your default values, as there may a need for you to improve some of them.

Generating Asset Directory Contents

Now that we have the file "cluster.yaml," we can generate the assets based on it. This is shown below:

```
$kube-aws render
WARNING: The generated client TLS CA cert expires in 3650 days and the server and client cert expire in 365 days. It is recommended that you create your own TLS infrastructure for revocation and rotation of keys before using in prod

Success! Stack rendered to stack-template.json.

Next steps:
1. (Optional) Validate your changes to cluster.yaml with "kube-aws validate"

2. (Optional) Further customize the cluster by modifying stack-template.json or files in ./userdata.

3. Start the cluster with "kube-aws up".
```

As shown in the above case, we have generated some assets by use of the new random CA. However, this one is not good for use in production environments, and that is why we recommend that you make use of own PKI stack. The validation of the results can be done as shown below:

$kube-aws validate
Validating UserData...
UserData is valid.

Validating stack template...
Validation Report: {
Capabilities: ["CAPABILITY_IAM"],
CapabilitiesReason: "The following resource(s) require capabilities: [AWS::IAM::Role]",

Description: "kube-aws Kubernetes cluster kube-dev"
}
stack template is valid.
Validation OK!

You can then go ahead and run the following command:

kube-aws up

Using new cluster

For you to be able to use the new cluster, you must begin by setting the "kubectl" tool. This tool is part of the kubernetes and you can download it by running the following command:

$ wget https://github.com/kubernetes/kubernetes/blob/master/CHANGELOG.md#downloads-for-v145

The package comes in a zipped format, so you have to unzip it by running the command given below:

$ tar xzf kubernetes-client-linux-amd64.tar.gz
$ sudo cp kubernetes/client/bin/kubectl /usr/local/bin/kubectl

$ sudo chmod +x /usr/local/bin/kubectl

Note that after unzipping the file, we copied it to a new directory. We have then executed the file which installed it into our system. At this point, we have the kubectl tool installed into the system.

Since it has been installed in the directory having the cluster data, we can use it for the purpose of printing the node list of this cluster. This can be done as follows:

$kubectl --kubeconfig=kubeconfig get nodes
NAME STATUS AGE
Ip-10-0-0-125.eu-central-1.compute.internal
Ready 1h
Ip-10-0-0-50.eu-central-1.compute.internal
Ready,SchedulingDisabled 1h

If you need to destroy your kubernetes cluster, you only have to execute the command given below:

kube-aws up

Chapter 5- Running CoreOS on OpenStack

In this chapter, we will discuss how to download CoreOS for OpenStack, import the OpenStack with "glance," and then start the first CoreOS cluster with "nova" tool.

Uploading the Image

We will be using the OpenStack Docker CLI Image which provides us with the glance and nova tools. After connecting to the OpenStack, we can go ahead to download the CoreOS image. This comes in a zipped format, so we will have to unzip it. The following two commands can help us achieve this:

```
# download a stable channel
$ wget http://stable.release.core-os.net/amd64-usr/current/coreos_production_openstack_image.img.bz2

# extract the image
$ bunzip2 coreos_production_openstack_image.img.bz2
```

Now that we have downloaded and extracted the image, we can use the "glance" tool so as to upload it:

```
$ glance image-create --name CoreOS \
 --container-format bare \
 --disk-format qcow2 \
 --progress \
 --file coreos_production_openstack_image.img \
 --is-public True
```

You will then have uploaded the image to the glance. You should then go ahead and verify whether the upload was successful or not. You only have to run the following command:

```
$ glance image-list
```

It will be time for you to retrieve a new discovery token for your CoreOS cluster. Remember that we have used the etcd cluster which is provided by the CoreOS so as to manage our cluster. This makes it easy for the quickstart of the CoreOS cluster. Run the following command so as to request a new cluster token:

$ curl -w "\n" 'https://discovery.etcd.io/new?size=3'

The cloud config file

Create a local file named "cloud-config.yaml," and then replace https://discovery.etcd.io/<token> with the discovery URL you have obtained. This is shown below:

```
#cloud-config

coreos:
  etcd:
    # generate a new token for each unique cluster
from https://discovery.etcd.io/new?size=3

    # specify the intial size of your cluster with ?size=X
    discovery: https://discovery.etcd.io/<token>
    # multi-region and multi-cloud deployments need
to use $public_ipv4

    addr: $private_ipv4:4001
    peer-addr: $private_ipv4:7001
  units:
    - name: etcd.service
      command: start
    - name: fleet.service
      command: start
ssh_authorized_keys:
  # include one or more SSH public keys
```

- ssh-rsa ACABB3NzaC1yc2EAABCDAQABAAABAQDog+ZYxC7 weoIJLUafOgrm+j...

Creating new CoreOS Cluster

Now that our cloud-init file is ready, we can use "nova" so as to launch a 3-instance cluster.

There may be a need for you to adopt some security group names or flavor for the setup. This is shown below:

```
nova boot \
--user-data ./cloud-config.yaml \
--image CoreOS \
--key-name coreos \
--flavor m1.medium \
--num-instances 3 \
--security-groups default coreos
```

Once the command runs successfully, all the three instances will be available and ready in the OpenStack. You can verify this by running the command given below:

```
$ nova list
```

We should now go ahead and verify whether or not the CoreOS cluster has been registered with the fleet. First, runs the following command so as to SSH into the CoreOS:

```
ssh core@185.27.183.99
```

Next, do some verification to be sure that all the nodes have been properly registered in the fleet. You just have to run the command given below:

```
$ fleetctl list-machines
```

If you find that it has been registered, just know that your CoreOS cluster is currently running on the OpenStack.

Chapter 6- How to Deploy Web Apps in CoreOS

When using CoreOS to deploy your apps, very less configuration will be needed. Let us discuss how one can deploy their web app into the CoreOS.

First, begin by creating a unique key for your machine. This will help us keep each machine secure as it will have a security key. To create the key, run the following command:

```
ssh-keygen -t rsa -b 4096 -C "some comment"
```

Once you run the above command, a new SSH key will be created, and you can save it as "id_rsa." The content of "id_rsa.pub" will be given to the DigitalOcean when the server is being created. Once the server has been created, just verify to be sure that you are able to login:

```
ssh -i ./id_rsa core@<ip_address>
```

Setting up the Server

For you to make the script to be more reusable, create the "ipaddr.sh" as follows:

```
# e.g. IPADDR=137.62.26.191
IPADDR=<ip address of your server>
```

A kernel will always benefit from some tweaks. This is why you should create the "initial-server-setup.sh" and then run it first:

```
#!/bin/bash

set -u -e -o pipefail

. ./ipaddr.sh

ssh -i ./id_rsa core@${IPADDR} <<'ENDSSH'
```

```
# https://coreos.com/os/docs/latest/other-settings.html

sudo bash -c "echo net.netfilter.nf_conntrack_max=131072 > /etc/sysctl.d/nf.conf"

sudo sysctl --system
ENDSSH
```

When you run the above commands, then the number of the concurrent tcp connections will be increased.

We can then make use of the "systemctld" for the purpose of restarting the app automatically. Our aim is to have the app to be started automatically after the server has rebooted. The app should also restart automatically whenever it has crashed. We will make use of the "system" which comes with the CoreOS.

Create the file named "blog.service" and then instruct the sytemd on how it should run the Docker container by the name "blog." This is shown below:

```
# put in /etc/systemd/system/blog.service
[Unit]
Description=blog
# this unit will start after the docker.service
After=docker.service
Requires=docker.service

[Service]
TimeoutStartSec=0
EnvironmentFile=/etc/environment
# before starting make sure it doesn't exist
# '=-' means it can fail
ExecStartPre=-/usr/bin/docker rm blog
ExecStart=/usr/bin/docker run --rm -p 80:80 -v /data-blog:/data --name blog blog:latest
```

```
ExecStop=/usr/bin/docker stop blog
# restart if it fails or it is killed
Restart=on-failure
RestartSec=5

[Install]
WantedBy=multi-user.target
```

This is a one-time operation, but it is good for you to have this in the form of a script by the name "install-service.sh." This is shown below:

```
#!/bin/bash
set -u -e -o pipefail

. ./ipaddr.sh

scp -i ./id_rsa ./blog.service
core@${IPADDR}:/home/core/blog.service

ssh -i ./id_rsa core@${IPADDR} <<'ENDSSH'
cd /home/core
sudo cp blog.service /etc/systemd/system
sudo systemctl enable
/etc/systemd/system/blog.service
rm blog.service
ENDSSH
```

Once the .service has been updated, you should go ahead and re-run it. The app should then be packaged like a Docker image and then upload its latest version to your server. The docker registry is the best device for the purpose of uploading and downloading the docker images. To make it simple, you should use the "docker save/docker load" and the "scp."Here is the script for "docker_build_and_upload.sh":

```
#!/bin/bash

set -u -e -o pipefail
```

```
. ./ipaddr.sh

dir=`pwd`
blog_dir=${GOPATH}/src/github.com/dsv/blog

echo "building"
cp config.json "${blog_dir}"
cd "${blog_dir}"
GOOS=linux GOARCH=amd64 go build -o blog_linux
docker build --no-cache --tag blog:latest .
rm blog_linux
cd "${dir}"

echo "docker save"
docker save blog:latest | bzip2 > blog-latest.tar.bz2
ls -lah blog-latest.tar.bz2

echo "uploading to the server"
scp -i ./id_rsa blog-latest.tar.bz2
core@${IPADDR}:/home/core/blog-latest.tar.bz2

echo "extracting on the server"
ssh -i ./id_rsa core@${IPADDR} <<'ENDSSH'
cd /home/core
bunzip2 --stdout blog-latest.tar.bz2 | docker load
rm blog-latest.tar.bz2
sudo systemctl restart blog
ENDSSH

rm -rf blog-latest.tar.bz2
```

Now that you have set everything okay, just restart the OS by running the “shutdown –r” command.

This will help you verify whether the app starts up after the reboot. It will also be good for you to write the “login.sh” as shown below:

```
#!/bin/bash
../ipaddr.sh
ssh -i ./id_rsa core@${IPADDR}
```

You can also write the "tail-logs.s" file as shown below:

```
#!/bin/bash
../ipaddr.sh
ssh -i ./id_rsa core@${IPADDR} <<'ENDSSH'
cd /home/core
docker logs -f blog
ENDSSH
```

Chapter 7- Load Balancing

It is possible for you to create an effective load balancing arrangement in the CoreOS by use of confd and nginx while running from separate containers. In this chapter, we will guide you on how to balance multiple web application containers using nginx across a cluster of the machines which use CoreOS.

We will be creating the following:

1. An Apache container which will represent our app. This will register itself with the etcd so as to allow all the available containers to be discovered.

2. A data volume which can be written by the confgd.

3. A container which runs confgd. This will watch for the changes in the etcd and build a nginx configuration file for load balancing among the available containers.

4. An nginx container having its configuration from the shared volume.

Once this setup is completed, it will be easy for you to add some new Apache containers, and these will be automatically added to the load-balancing background.

The Apache Container

We want to begin from the bottom while going up. This is expected to act as the backend for our application.

For the docker image to be deployed into the CoreOS cluster, we should first define the fleet service. This will be named "apache.service" with the following code:

[Unit]

Description=Basic port for web service %i
After=docker.service
Requires=docker.service

[Service]
EnvironmentFile=/etc/environment
ExecStartPre=-/usr/bin/docker kill apache-%i
ExecStartPre=-/usr/bin/docker rm apache-%i
ExecStartPre=/usr/bin/docker pull nicohsam/hello-world

ExecStartPre=/usr/bin/etcdctl set /test/apache-%i ${COREOS_PRIVATE_IPV4}:%i

ExecStart=/usr/bin/docker run --rm --name apache-%i -p ${COREOS_PRIVATE_IPV4}:%i:80 nicohsam/hello-world

ExecStop=/usr/bin/etcdctl rm /test/apache-%i
ExecStop=/usr/bin/docker stop -t 3 apache-%i

Just save the file as "apache.service," then go ahead to create two symlinks by the name "apache@8001.service" and "apache@8002.service."

When it comes to the unit file, the placeholder "%i" will be replaced with text after @. After running the apache@8001.service, it will begin by pulling the /etc/environment. It will then trio to kill then remove any container named "apache-8001."

The exposed port and the IP address of the apache container which is to be started into the "/test/apache-8001" etcd key. This will make it for discovery of newly minted container. The Apache container will then be started. Let us now use fleetctl so as to start the two apache units:

fleetctl start apache@8001.service
fleetctl start apache@8002.service

We can confirm the machines in which the units have been started:

fleetctl list-units

The units will then be listed. The "etcdctl" can help us to list the keys which were created by the units:

etcdctl ls /test
/test/apache-8001
/test/apache-8002

We can choose one of those units, inspect it, and then see the port and IP address it is exposing. This is shown below:

etcdctl get /test/apache-8001
172.17.8.102:8001

At this point, it is possible for us to create as many apache containers as we want, and these will automatically announce themselves to the etcd.

confd data volume

The confd is just a daemon which can be configured so that it can show made to the etcd keys and the configuration files will be generated from the template files which have been filled with the current etcd values.

Since the files are being shared between two containers, there is a need for a data volume. Below is the code for the file "confdata.service" which helps us create a data volume:

[Unit]
Description=Configuration Data Volume Service
After=docker.service
Requires=docker.service

```
[Service]
Type=oneshot
RemainAfterExit=yes

ExecStartPre=-/usr/bin/docker rm conf-data
ExecStart=/usr/bin/docker run -v /etc/nginx --name
conf-data nginx echo "created new data container"
```

You should ensure that you made it to be a one shot unit. The unit will clear the volume in case it exists, and a new container will be created.

We can now use fleetctl so as to start the confdata.service. A container named conf-data will be created, and this will provide us with some place for storage of the nginx configuration. You just have the following two commands:

```
fleetctl start confdata.service
fleetctl list-units
```

This will give us somewhere for writing the nginx configuration.

confd-demo container

We need to create a new image for running confd, so you just have to create a new directory having a Docker file shown below:

```
FROM ubuntu:14.04
RUN apt-get update && \
  DEBIAN_FRONTEND=noninteractive apt-get -y
install curl && \

  curl -o /usr/bin/confd -L
https://github.com/kelseyhightower/confd/releases/
download/v0.7.1/confd-0.7.1-linux-amd64 && \
```

```
chmod 755 /usr/bin/confd && \
curl -sSL https://get.docker.com/ubuntu/ | sh

ADD etc/confd/ /etc/confd

CMD /usr/bin/confd -interval=60 -
node=http://$COREOS_PRIVATE_IPV4:4001
```

The above just works to install a binary release of the confd. It will also install the Docker for you.

Other than the Docker file, you should create the directory etc/confd as it will give us storage for the confd configurations and the templates.

The startup command will start the confd. An interval of 10 minutes forms the default for checking of the etcd, but this has been changed to a minute.

The file "confd/etcd/confd/conf.d/nginx.toml" will be responsible for telling the confd about the keys which need to be watched, and the actions to be taken in case a change is needed. This is shown below:

```
[template]
src = "nginx.conf.tmpl"
dest = "/etc/nginx/nginx.conf"
keys = [
  "/test",
]
reload_cmd = "/usr/bin/docker kill -s HUP
nginx.service"
```

Once our confd has changed the configuration of nginx, our need is for the nginx to begin using it. The nginx will have to reload the configuration, once a HUP signal is received, and the Docker is aware of how to send signals to the containers.

confd/etcd/confd/templates/nginx.conf.tmpl

The last part of the container image should be a template for configuration of the nginx. The following are the template directives to be executed by the confide. They will iterate over the keys contained in /test/ and then use values contained in those keys for definition of backend servers:

```
upstream backend {
    {{range getvs "/test/*"}}
      server {{.}};
    {{end}}
  }
```

The full configuration should be as follows:

```
user  nginx;
worker_processes  1;

error_log  /var/log/nginx/error.log warn;
pid        /var/run/nginx.pid;

events {
  worker_connections  1024;
}

http {
  include       /etc/nginx/mime.types;
  default_type  application/octet-stream;

  log_format  main  '$remote_addr - $remote_user
[$time_local] "$request" '
```

```
            '$status $body_bytes_sent "$http_referer"
'
            '"$http_user_agent"
"$http_x_forwarded_for"';

    access_log  /var/log/nginx/access.log  main;

    sendfile        on;
    #tcp_nopush     on;

    keepalive_timeout  65;

    #gzip  on;

    upstream backend {
      {{range getvs "/test/*"}}
        server {{.}};
      {{end}}
    }

    server {
      server_name www.sample.com;

      location / {
        proxy_pass http://backend;
        proxy_redirect off;
        proxy_set_header Host $host;
        proxy_set_header X-Real-IP $remote_addr;
        proxy_set_header X-Forwarded-For
$proxy_add_x_forwarded_for;

        add_header  X-Handler  $upstream_addr;
      }
    }
    include /etc/nginx/conf.d/*.conf;
}
```

At this point, we have the Docker file, the nginx configuration file, and the nginx confd template, so we can go ahead and create the confd container image as follows:

```
CONFD_CONTAINER="username/demo-confd"
docker build --tag="$CONFD_CONTAINER" .
docker push $CONFD_CONTAINER
```

A fleet unit can then be defined for the purpose of running the container image. The confd.service should have the code given below:

```
[Unit]
Description=Configuration Service
After=confdata.service
Requires=confdata.service

[Service]
EnvironmentFile=/etc/environment

#kill any existing confd
ExecStartPre=-/usr/bin/docker kill %n
ExecStartPre=-/usr/bin/docker rm %n

ExecStart=/usr/bin/docker run --rm \
  -e
COREOS_PRIVATE_IPV4=${COREOS_PRIVATE_IP
V4} \

  -v /var/run/docker.sock:/var/run/docker.sock \
  --volumes-from=conf-data \
  --name %n \
  username/demo-confd
```

We have created an environment variable named "COREOS_PRIVATE_IPV4" which should be a copy from "/etc/environment" variable. This will be used by the Dockerfile for telling the container the location of etcd. The docker socket should be mounted from a host inside our container.

After starting the service, you will find it scheduled on the same machine as the conf-data.service. You can go ahead and peek the data volume by launching the shell in a temporary container and grepping the config file so as to be sure this worked. This is shown below:

```
docker run --rm -ti --volumes-from=conf-data nginx \
 grep -A6 'upstream backend' /etc/nginx/nginx.conf
  upstream backend {

        server 172.17.8.102:8001;

        server 172.17.8.103:8002;

  }
```

Nginx container

We should now get our nginx up and running. We are making use of a public nginx container.

So far, we have not used requires=confd.service, since a restart or a stop on confd should not start the nginx. The nginx.service should be as follows:

```
[Unit]
Description=Nginx Service
After=confd.service
#Requires=confd.service
[Service]
```

```
EnvironmentFile=/etc/environment
ExecStartPre=-/usr/bin/docker kill %n
ExecStartPre=-/usr/bin/docker rm %n
ExecStartPre=/usr/bin/docker pull nginx
ExecStart=/usr/bin/docker run --name %n -p 80:80 --
volumes-from=conf-data nginx

ExecStop=/usr/bin/docker stop -t 3 %n
Restart=on-failure

[X-Fleet]
MachineOf=confdata.service
```

You should also note that just like the confd, the unit has been constrained so that it can run on a similar machine as your data volume. Just run the following commands:

```
fleetctl start nginx.service
fleetctl list-units
```

Conclusion

We have come to the end of this book. CoreOS is a Linux distribution which helps you to setup a clustered environment in your system. The good thing with this distribution is that you can set it up in a public, private, or in a virtual environment. Once you setup a cluster within the CoreOS environment, your operations are made easier. You will be able to run multiple complex applications simultaneously in your machine. A good example of this is Node.js.

You can install Node.js and run it in a CoreOS cluster. When you setup clusters in your CoreOS system, it will be easy for you to manage them. This is because all of these clusters can be managed as a single unit. This means that we will be able to run multiple operations at once with minimal or no overhead. This is what each one desires to have. We can also deploy our web apps on CoreOS and run them from there. This is because you can install Nginx, which is a web server, in the CoreOS system.

www.ingramcontent.com/pod-product-compliance
Lightning Source LLC
Chambersburg PA
CBHW070901070326
40690CB00009B/1939

* 9 7 8 1 5 4 6 4 9 4 1 6 4 *